Destiny
MOMENTS

LaMonika N. Jones

Limits of Liability and Disclaimer of Warranty

The author and publisher shall not be liable for your misuse of this material. This book is strictly for informational and educational purposes. The purpose of this book is to educate and entertain. The author and/or publisher do not guarantee that anyone following these techniques, suggestions, tips, ideas, or strategies will become successful. The author and/or publisher shall have neither liability nor responsibility to anyone with respect to any loss or damage caused, or alleged to be caused, directly or indirectly by the information contained in this book.

Views expressed in this publication do not necessarily reflect the views of the publisher.

Book Cover Design: Studio 5 Agency
Photography: Anthony Thomas Photography

Printed in the United States of America
ISBN: 978-0-9990740-0-8

Keen Vision Publishing, LLC
www.keen-vision.com

destined /ˈdestined/

Adjective: Bound for a certain (destination)
1. (of a person's future) Developing as according to plan
2. Certain to meet a particular fate

Verb
1. To be set apart for a particular use, purpose, etc.
2. To appoint or ordain beforehand; as by divine decree; fore ordain; predetermine.

Acknowledgements

Over the years, God has given me so many destiny moments. I am grateful for these moments because they have brought us closer together. God, thank you so much for being patient, loving, and understanding as I grow. Along the way, God has blessed me with some amazing individuals who have loved, supported, and pushed me to become the woman I am today. Mom, Dad, & Brandon, thank you for always being my biggest cheerleaders! You all are my greatest support system. You continue to allow me to grow and mature into the woman God has created me to be. God has blessed me beyond measure by bringing us together as a family. I love you!

My sweetheart, Bria, though you're only four years old, you have brought me so much joy. When you grow up, I pray you follow the destiny God has placed before you. Tee Tee loves you immensely!

To my ever-expanding circle of friends and supporters, I thank each and every one of you for propelling me into the place I am now. Each of you continues to play an active role in shaping who I am becoming. I thank God for our destiny moments because that is what has brought us together. Thank you for being patient, loving, and understanding as I grow!

Finally, to you, the reader. Thank you so much for supporting this book. I pray that it helps you understand your purpose and sets you on a path of fulfilling your God-given destiny!

About the Author

LaMonika is currently a Purchasing Manager for a leading Metro Atlanta Minority Women Owned Small Business. Her passion for education, social activism, and youth empowerment led to her completion of a Master's Degree in Urban Teacher Leadership with emphasis on Middle-Level Education. LaMonika has worked to research and provide solutions on how to improve schooling for adults and children in rural and urban America. Her desire to transform the face of education has paired her with individuals in the forefront of education reform such as Former State Representative and Current Executive Director for Ivy Preparatory Academy Alisha Thomas Morgan, with whom she served as a Legislative Intern. LaMonika is an exemplary servant in her community having worked with non-profit organizations such as Juvenile Diabetes Research Foundation (JDRF) serving on their Young Leaders Committee (YLC), Passion for Life, Atlanta Glow, etc. When not serving, LaMonika can be found expressing her thoughts via her blog www.lamonikanicole.com.

Contents

Introduction

We are all destined to become something. Whether we walk in the fullness of our earthly assignments depends on how well we understand our destiny. Life is inevitably going to happen, but how well we maneuver and navigate through the tough seasons depend on our willingness to press in and stay focused on the goal.

To come to the realization of what we are destined to become, we must first attack our fears, embrace our challenges, and acknowledge the greatness God poured into us the very moment we were created. In this book, we will break down what it means to be destined, the purpose God has for our lives, the courage to walk into our destiny as well as the importance of connection, uniqueness, and the role people play in our destiny.

My desire for this book is for every person to arrive at a place of understanding – understanding that they indeed have a purpose and are destined for greatness. My goal is for every reader to view themselves as an overcomer; gifted with the power to break through their struggles and walk in the full manifestation of their destiny.

Life isn't easy but must endure if we desire to win the prize. To do this, it's imperative that we move past our fears and mistakes and move into victory. The moment has come for us to shake off the excuses. Now is the time to get busy and pursue destiny! What are you waiting for?

Chapter One

Destiny's Child

My Destiny Moment: *College Graduate. Full-Time Job. Debt Free. Unhappy. Unsatisfied.*

The year was 2005, and I had just graduated college. After five years of studying to become an attorney, I was beyond excited to be finished. I completed my undergraduate degree in Political Science & Communication, and I was ready to attack my LSAT and head to law school. As I began to prepare for my entrance exam and complete law school applications, I started to question if I was making the right choice. On paper and in conversation, my plans seemed great. I would attend Howard University School of Law, pass my bar exam, become a Federal Prosecutor in Washington, DC, and finally become the 1st African American Female on the Supreme Court. Everything seemed well except I wasn't sure if this was the 'perfect plan.'

My 'Type A' personality has been in operation since I was a child. I'm known to focus on a goal and work until it's achieved. I'm talking a real life, Philippians 3:12 mindset. All my life, I'd only wanted to be an attorney. If anyone were to ask what I wanted to be when I grew up, the answer was always: an attorney. During my scholarship interviews, the future career questions were always answered with Federal Prosecutor followed by Supreme Court Justice – as if there were any other career options. However, when the time came to put the plan into action, I stalled. I was no longer confident this was the career God destined for me to obtain. Nonetheless, I took my exam and applied to law school. Everyone was excited and happy, except me. Deep down, I knew there was something else. I just didn't know what it was or how to unearth it.

DESTINY

Many of us are traveling through space in time not knowing that we were created for more in life. Some of us are focusing on a goal that will only satisfy our "right now." We were created for much more than just our "right now" phase. How do we discover the future? How do we get to the place where we are operating in our tomorrow and not just our today? It starts with definition. We must define our destiny. Merriam-Webster defines destiny as the future; the things someone or something will experience in the future; or, a predetermined course of events. Webster's 1828 Dictionary defines destiny as the state or condition of something that is predetermined; an ultimate fate; the fixed order of things established by a divine decree. The author confirms in Ecclesiastes 6:10 the existence of our destiny. God predetermined our future.

Our lives were mapped out prior to us being birthed from our mother's womb. When He looked upon us, He pointed to our future. He did not simply speak to the child that was in front of Him. He spoke to the person we would become in the future. Before we can march into our purpose or create our vision boards, we must first come to the revelation that God has a future for us. We should rest knowing that the future God has for us is brighter than anything we could ever image for ourselves. We must rest in the understanding that we do have a future, we are going places, we are connecting with people, and we are impacting lives. Ecclesiastes 6:10 (NLT) says, *"Everything has already been decided. It was known long ago what each person would be. So there' s no use in arguing with God about your destiny."*

PURPOSE

As we come into the knowledge that we were created with a destiny, we cannot define our destiny without defining our purpose. Our purpose is what leads us into destiny. Once we uncover our purpose, we can then begin to walk into our destiny. Webster's 1828 Dictionary defines 'purpose' as that which a person sets before himself as an object to be reached or accomplished. Purpose is also defined as intention or being designed/built for a particular use. The Bible highlights the importance of purpose by saying this, "But I have spared you for a purpose – to show you my power and to spread my fame throughout the earth" Exodus 9:16 (NLT). When trying to arrive at our purpose, we must understand that God intentionally created us. We must attempt to understand the why behind His actions and what our purpose should accomplish. Completing these tasks requires us to spend time in the Word of God. To learn how something works, we must first read the manual. If we want to know how God operates, we must spend time with Him via prayer and His Word.

Now you may be saying to yourself, "I've spent time in God's Word, and I've prayed, but what actions do I take to discover my purpose?" The first thing we must do is define the word, purpose. When it comes to discovering our purpose, sometimes we must look at the end before focusing on the beginning. A beneficial question to ask is what exactly is the problem (acknowledging there is a problem). Next, we should create a strategy plan on how to alleviate the problem and ultimately what can we do to be a part of the solution. For example, if we identify the problem as an increase in school violence, the next step would be to create a solution such as prayer in school. We could then ask ourselves: What can I do to restore prayer and harmony within school districts? From this observation, one may discover their purpose is to advocate for children. As you continue to walk in your purpose, God will continue to add layers. The first layer may be student advocacy, but the next layer could involve advocacy for the church, and so on. Often it takes involving ourselves in various activities to discover our true design.

I used to work with middle and high school students helping them to discover their passion and purpose. The one question I would ask was: What would you do if money and time were not a factor? Once they arrived at their answer, we began the process of elimination as far as careers and interests to narrow down their passion. They were only middle and high school students. They had plenty of experiences to take advantage of, but it was essential for them to begin the process of tapping into their passion and understanding their purpose so they could begin their path to destiny.

As adults, we are no different than my students. Often, the first step in arriving at our purpose is to determine what we are passionate about. Our passions have the innate ability to point us in the direction of our purpose. When I began working with my students, I was fully devoted to a legal career. Along the way, my passion for law was coupled with a newly discovered passion for education, which then led to my purpose. It's key that we take time out to discover what we like, consult God, and allow Him to lead us down the path to purpose. Jeremiah 29:11(NLT) says, *"For I know the plans I have for you, says the Lord. They are plans for good and not for disaster, to give you a future and a hope."*

Sometimes our purpose does not look like what we imagined. We have a plan in our mind, have already started moving on the plan, but something tells us that the plan we have so diligently focused on is not God's plan. The beauty in that is realizing that God has created us for something better. Isaiah 55 reminds us that God's ways are higher than our ways; his thoughts are greater than our thoughts. As our master designer and as our potter, God has formed us into the very thing He needs us to be. Jeremiah 29 reminds us that God has a plan for us all. He has created us with purpose and with a plan that will prosper us and not bring disaster into our lives. The key is connecting with God and channeling into His wisdom so we can gain access to His plan.

DESTINY VS. PURPOSE

Hopefully, by now, you have a pretty solid understanding of destiny and purpose. The next question, perhaps, is how they differ. Do I have purpose and not a destiny? Can I have a destiny but not purpose? The answer to these questions is simple.

No. You have both. Destiny and purpose are not opposing forces, but rather complimentary powers that feed off one another. To walk into our destiny, we must have a clear understanding of our purpose. We cannot begin to walk into our future if we do not know where we are going. I cannot invite someone on vacation with me and not know our destination. Having a destiny and walking in the full manifestation of that destiny requires us to know where we are going. We may not know how we are going to get there, but at least we know where we are going and why.

Destiny Steps

Ask Yourself...

- Do I understand what it means to have purpose?
- Am I purposeful?
- What am I doing to begin walking into my purpose?
- What can I do to begin walking into my purpose?
- If money and time were not a factor, what would I want to spend my time doing?

YOUR DESTINY MOMENT

Spend some time thinking about the issues and concerns in your life that are most bothersome. Think about how you can create a solution to the issues facing your world. Remember, your purpose is bigger than you. Step outside of the box and ponder on how your purpose can benefit the next generation.

Chapter Two

Imago Dei

My Destiny Moment: *Confused. Uninspired.*
Hopeless. Empty.

On October 13, 2008, I quit my job, packed all of my belongings, and moved to Atlanta, GA. What did I have to lose? NOT A THING!! Although I had taken my LSAT and began the application process for law school, something was missing. God had continuously been tugging at my heart, but I ignored the calls. It had been awhile since I actively attended church, but I knew the tugging was because I needed to re-establish my relationship with Christ. I needed to re-connect with God because He ultimately had what I needed to restore my hope. God had the understanding I needed to fully walk into my destiny. The disconnection hindered me from accurately discerning the voice of God. Moving to Atlanta and removing myself from what was familiar created a space for me to be alone with God. It allowed me to commune with Him in a private space with no distractions. I had nothing: no job, no friends, no purpose (so I thought). It was just my apartment, God, and I. In that lonely, quiet space God slowly began to rework my life. He slowly began to undo the hopelessness, confusion, and discontent I had allowed to build up. God untied the knots in my heart and released reassurance, confidence, purpose, and destiny. He began to show me why I was created.

For many years, I walked around not knowing why I was created. I had no idea why I was birthed in this specific time and era. It was not until I fully dedicated my life to Christ that I began to understand why God had me here. Up until this point in my life, all I knew was I wanted to become a federal prosecutor and eventually a Supreme Court justice, but I could not answer why. When my best friend decided she wanted to attend law school to practice international law as a means to aid our nation's Hispanic immigrants, the first thought I had was, wow, she has such a clear perspective on her reason for wanting to become an attorney. I didn't have the same revelation. I wanted to attend law school, but I didn't know why. I couldn't say for sure that attending law school was my purpose. I couldn't answer how becoming a practicing attorney was going to point people closer to Christ. I spent much time questioning God. I asked Him how was it that others around me had a great understanding of their purpose, but I was still dazed and confused.

At this point in my life, God began to reveal His truest heart to me. God began to show me that the purpose He created me for was greater than anything I could ever imagine. I also began to study teachings by Dr. Myles Munroe. Through Dr. Munroe, I began to understand that my purpose involved much more than a professional title. I began to understand that my purpose would ultimately point people back to Christ. I began to realize that God created me to reach a particular generation and group of people. It began to register in my heart that God created me with a specific plan and future in mind.

Many of us walk around confused and uninspired. We have a misunderstanding that life consists of making as much money as possible, driving the best car, wearing the most expensive clothes, etc. We wander around the earth sightless, not realizing that life is much more precious than our tangible possessions. We do not realize that we are created with authority and have a responsibility to operate in authority. The same authority God created us with in Genesis 1:27, is the same authority we must tap into to uncover our purpose and begin our journey to destiny. We must remove the blindfolds that prohibit us from seeing ourselves as God sees us.

When God breathed life into us, He didn't breathe into us the mistakes of our past. He did not breathe into us failure. The very breath we have in our bodies is the breath of wholeness, fullness, and completeness. God sees each person on this earth as His masterpiece. We are intricately knit together and created to do great things. We were designed to accomplish what may seem incomprehensible and beyond our capability. God sees us as overcomers able to endure hardship and press on toward the goal He has before us. God handpicked each one of us delicately as if we were a rare flower. He has the ability to look past our faults and speak directly to the greatness lying dormant on the inside.

For some of us, it seems unimaginable that God would pick someone as lowly as we are to accomplish something so great and so big. The reality is, it's not unimaginable – it's conceivable! We only view it as such because we do not truly understand the desire of God's heart.

We must understand that God desires outweigh any insecurity we may have. What sense does it make for an engineer to design a car with the capability to fly, but the car never leaves the ground? That makes no sense! The car is not being used according to the engineer's original design or to the capacity in which it was created; the car is being limited. We limit ourselves in the same manner when we do not come to understand the complete desire of God's heart. When we choose to live life according to our limitations, it limits the power God has to work in our lives. Living a limited life is like telling God, "I know your desires, but I'm okay with doing just enough." Who wants to live in the "just enough"? NOT ME! I'd rather live in the overflowing abundance of God's desires. For a meat eater, it's like passing up prime rib and settling for tofu. We have to move past our limitations and step into greatness if we truly want to experience the desires of God's heart and begin the journey to destiny.

Destiny Steps

Ask Yourself…

- Do I understand why I was created?
- How does God see me?
- Do the desires of my heart match the desires of God?
- What can I do to ensure my desires are God's desires?

YOUR DESTINY MOMENT

Take a few moments to ponder on the image of God and how His creation of mankind shapes your destiny. Reflect on God's original design for man and the purpose He created him for. Meditate on the Bible verses below (Joshua 1:8) and allow yourself to fully come to an understanding about how God's sees you and the desires He has for your life.

- Esther 4:14
- Psalm 139:14
- Ephesians 2:10

Chapter Three
The Elsa Effect

My Destiny Moment: *Acceptance. Understanding. Forgiveness. Freedom.*

Living on your own and away from the life you were accustomed to forces you to do a lot of reflection. After finally settling in my new city and becoming more and more acclimated to life in the south, God began to peel back the layers of my life. He slowly began to show me my ways and how I interacted with other people. This was NOT fun. He also began to reveal to me the woman He called me to be. Piece-by-piece, layer-by-layer, God began to infuse His ways into my heart. There was a renewal happening in my life. This renewal was one that only came the moment I accepted what God had to say about me. As I began to lean into God's teachings and studied more of His word, the more my heart began to transform into the woman He destined for me to be. God began to work out of me old ways of thinking and impart into me new understandings. Take a moment to think of the road to Damascus where God stepped in and intervened with the Apostle Paul's life. Paul (Saul at the time) was on a destructive path when God said to him, "Okay. Enough is enough. Now is the time for you to leave the life you are living and begin walking in the destiny I have for you." God began to peel back the layers of Paul's life layer-by-layer to reveal his destiny. Paul's Damascus experience was designed for Paul to step into freedom. It was the place where Paul was set free from his past and launched into his future. This is the place where Paul gave God his all. After being broken down and stripped of everything familiar, Paul could see his life according to God's original intent. It was not until I had my very own "Damascus Road" moment that I could give God all of me and walk in complete freedom and forgiveness.

Just like the Apostle Paul, my "Damascus Road" moment involved redirection. God not only had to redirect my path, but He also had to redirect my steps. For God's will to be done, I had to be willing to open myself up to who God was calling me to be. Paul had to believe that God's will for him was better than the path he was currently traveling. This was the only way Paul could understand the destiny God had planned for him. There had to be a physical, spiritual, and emotional exchange - the old for the new. Sometimes, we are not able to fully accept our destiny because we do not believe God has a destiny mapped out for us. Maybe you want to believe God has a destiny for you, but you struggle with complete revelation and understanding of God's destiny. To accept what God is saying as the truth, there must be a renewing of the mind. We must purge our mind of the old way of thinking. We must completely do away with the thought that we are not destined to be We must intentionally adapt to God's way of thinking. For some of us, this may introduce another question, "How do I renew my mind?" Jude 20 admonishes us to build ourselves on our most holy faith. Romans 10:17 teaches us that faith comes by hearing and hearing by the Word of God. So, to renew our mind and build ourselves, we must read the Word of God and meditate on it day and night. Referencing our Word gives us the ability to undo the tangles in our hearts and knots in our minds that prevent us from discovering and walking into our destiny.

Once we are walking with a renewed mind, we can operate in freedom. We experience freedom by letting go of the old and embracing the new with little to no care.

I'm sure we are all familiar with Disney's favorite princess, Queen Elsa. In the movie, Frozen, Elsa struggled with the reality of her icy super power. She was bound by the fear of just how powerful she was and the damage that could be done. She knew there was greatness locked on the inside of her, but because she was afraid of the power she held, she remained in a self-imposed prison. Elsa's fear of her superpower held more weight in her mind than the belief that her super powers were meant for good. It wasn't until she renewed her mind to believe her power was designed to help people that she actually used them to do so. The renewing of her mind allowed her to walk in freedom and into her destiny.

Like Elsa, many of us have super powers (gifts and calling from God), but we are not accepting of the way God sees us. We also refuse to walk in the freedom that comes with renewing our mind, letting go of our past and walking into the destiny God has prepared for us. The longer we hold on to our fears, mistakes, and old ways of thinking, the longer we prolong our steps toward destiny. Like Elsa, we must LET IT GO! We must see beyond ourselves. We must look past our fears and utilize the super powers God gave us.

For some of us, the prolonging of our destiny is not due to a lack of mind renewal, but instead, a lack of forgiveness. I can vividly remember the day I sat on the edge of my bed and asked God why couldn't I move beyond this particular area in my life. Sweetly and softly, as only God knows how, He told me I had not forgiven the people in my life nor had I forgiven myself. When I moved to Atlanta, I expected God to point me in the path of my purpose, but I did not know that path would include forgiveness. I was sure I had forgiven two specific people. God quickly revealed to me that I hadn't forgiven them. Since they were out of my sight, they were out of my mind. As I sat on my bed, I allowed the Holy Spirit to walk me through previous years' scenarios where I had not forgiven but rather pushed the pain to the back of my mind. While I was over the situations, I had not fully relinquished the power these situations had over my life. I allowed God to take the pain, hurt, anger, confusion, and every other emotion to the grave and bury it. I acknowledged my role and began to forgive myself. The forgiveness eventually led to healing and restoration.

When we look at our situations, the realization of the matter is that we are coping instead of dealing with the root of our issues. We are packing away our hurt and pain in storage bins, placing them in the attic of our minds, and hoping no one will discover them. For many of us, our next destiny step requires us to forgive some people and ourselves. Forgiving others allows us to give God the clearance to launch us into the next steps of our destiny. We free ourselves of the past and open ourselves up to the future.

Destiny Steps

Ask Yourself…

- Am I harboring any un-forgiveness?
- Have I truly renewed my mind to the idea of a destiny designed by God?
- Do I whole-heartedly accept who God says I am?
- Am I ready to LET IT GO to walk in my destiny?

YOUR DESTINY MOMENT

Think about who God says you are. Walk in agreement with God according to the person He has called you to be. Make this confession:

I am destined by God to become the very image of God. I walk in forgiveness daily. I accept the plans and purposes God has ordained for my life. I am renewing my mind daily to Word of God and committing myself to hearing the Word to develop my faith. I fully accept God's calling and destiny for my life.

Chapter Four

S. O. S

My Destiny Moment: Surrender. Obedience.
Submission

've always been the strong-willed child in my house. I felt the need to do things my way with little input from others. I've always respected authority, but I still found a "work-around" to do things my way. I can remember countless times telling my younger brother what to do and my mother swiftly reminding me that I was not his mother. Moving to Atlanta and completely surrendering my life to Christ was a bit of a challenge. For the first time in my adult life, I had to fully surrender myself to someone else. This surrender required me to let go of my way of thinking and completely trust that someone would lead and guide me in a way that ensured and secured my future. This was not an easy task. God slowly walked me down a path of complete surrender, obedience, and submission (S.O.S). God revealed to me that S.O.S was a step-by-step process that first required me to surrender completely to Him. Once I surrendered, I could trust and be obedient to Him. God showed me what it meant to truly trust -- not just a simple kind of trust, but a complete overhaul of what I thought it meant to trust someone. He began to reveal that the people I thought I could trust, but eventually let me down were not perfect. God taught me that an imperfect person cannot be trusted the same way Christ can be trusted. God redefined trust by revealing His character and showing me that I could share with Him the deepest places in my heart. He assured me that I could trust Him with the places that hurt the most and showed me how He could help me. He is not a God that would lie. His word confirms it.

Through His guidance, I began to do simple things to allow myself to come to Him with my cares, concerns, and deepest issues. Each time, He would be there with a resolution. I eventually realized that the sooner I let go of my erratic, irrational, emotional, and unstable way of thinking, the sooner God could increase my steps and push me further into destiny. After trust and obedience, I could remain submitted to His will.

Surrender, obedience, and submission are words that cause most people to cringe when they hear them. We hear the word surrender and automatically think defeat, but that's not the case with God. When we surrender our way of thinking and operating to God, we open to the beauty of perfection that has created a perfect pathway that only leads to success. To properly surrender, we must completely let go of our ways. We should acknowledge God for who He is --

all-knowing, all-powerful, supreme, and the head of our lives. The plans we have already constructed for our lives are no longer valid when we submit to God. There cannot be two plans in place when submitting to the Father; only one will win. If you are like me, trusting in yourself and only yourself has a high probability of failing. Why trust and surrender to something or someone that doesn't have the greatest track record? Why surrender to someone or something that hasn't stood the test of time?

If we are to surrender our lives to Christ, trust must be a factor. If we do not trust in the God we are surrendering to, there is no real reason to surrender. We might as well continue down the trial and error path we are traveling.

Someone may mention, "I want to surrender to God, I want to trust in Him, but I don't know how." In addition to trust, we must also be obedient to God. High school was a rocky phase for me. My name was synonymous with punishment, and my 16-year-old life would not come together. I wanted to have a life like most teenagers, but I could not get my attitude in check. This often landed me in trouble with my parents. They were strict, but also disciplinarians. Disobedience was not tolerated. If there was a future event I wanted to attend, I had to be obedient and follow the instructions they gave me including weekly chores, good grades, no talking back, etc. Now we all have a destiny, but if we want to avoid delays or being put on punishment by God, we must do what He tells us to do when He tells us to do it. With surrender comes obedience. We may have an idea in our mind of how we want to do something, but God has something different in mind. Again, surrendering to God requires us to be obedient.

So far, we have learned that when we surrender, we must be obedient. To be obedient, one must show submission. Merriam-Webster defines the word submit as to stop trying to fight or resist something; to agree to do or accept something that you have been resisting or opposing. Here is a question: How many of us are prolonging our destiny because we refuse to submit to the will of God? How many of us cannot get past our mistakes and failures because we refuse to submit to forgiveness and healing? If we want to make beneficial destiny steps, we must submit and stop resisting. Submission does not require us to give up the ability to think for ourselves or eliminate the power we obtain. Submission is an act of no longer resisting what God has designed for us. True submission is agreeing to walk in covenant, acknowledge God as the head, and be willing to exchange our plans for His plans. Submitting ourselves to God is submitting to our destiny. It is one of the most important components of our destiny. Submission recognizes Jesus as the way, the truth, and the life (John 14:6

NLT). Our submission allows us to admit that although we do not have the answers and do not know the next steps, we are yielding to the understanding that God knows exactly what He is doing. We may not believe we are good enough or that our skillset is up to par, but we place our hope & value in Christ and how He sees us.

During my own personal "journey to destiny," I had to be finite in my decision to trust God. I didn't think I was good enough to have a purpose. So many of my friends were walking into everything their hearts desired and everything I believed God purposed them to do. Yet, I didn't believe God had the same goals and plans prepared for me. Ultimately, I knew that if I wanted to walk in the greatness of God and become the woman God destined for me to be, I had to submit to His calling. I had to resist the thoughts that told me I wasn't going to become anything great or impact the world. I had to speak greatness over myself. I had to speak life, purpose, and gifting over myself. I had to renew my mind according to the Word of God and be obedient to what God asked me to do. I had to cast all my cares, fears, insecurities, and worries on Him. I had to REST NOT in my shortcomings, but in the value, purpose, and gifts God saw in me. If I rested in the areas in which I lacked, I would always lack and never move into the place God called me to be. The time has come for us to cancel out our way of thinking and be definitive in our choice to operate according to God's way and words.

Destiny Steps

Ask Yourself…

- Have I submitted myself to the person God has called me to be? Do I understand what it means to be submitted?
- How is my obedience? Have I completed the last thing God told me to do?
- Has my inability to be obedient, to surrender and to submit prevented me from taking more destiny steps?

YOUR DESTINY MOMENT

Now is your opportunity to align/realign yourself with Christ. Are there some missing pieces of the puzzle? Have you become sidetracked and missed an opportunity to hear God's instruction? Do you know how God speaks to you?

Take some time to determine the last thing God told you to do. If you did not complete the last thing God told you to do, go back and complete it. If you are having a hard time hearing the voice of God, get into a quiet space that is free from noise and distractions. Remember, God does not often speak in a loud booming voice from Heaven. He speaks in a small, quiet voice. If you are still having trouble discerning the voice of God from the voice of your spirit, remember the peace of God follows the will of God.

Wherever there is peace, God is amid it. Spend time meditating on this scripture:
"And the peace of God (that peace which reassures the heart, that peace) which transcends all understanding [that peace which] stands guard over your hearts and your minds in Christ Jesus [is yours]" Philippians 4:7 (Amplified)

Chapter Five
Pressure Cooker

My Destiny Moment: Pressure. Discipline. Patience.

A s I continued to journey through my new life in Atlanta, God slowly revealed His masterpiece puzzle. The more I continued to surrender my plans of becoming an attorney to God, the more He would reveal His desires for my life. As the revealing intensified, I realized I had to do some work. My destiny wasn't going to happen if I continued to rest on my laurels. I had to get up and do some work. In this space, I truly learned how lazy I could really be. I had to be honest with myself and admit to taking the easy route versus doing what may be difficult. For this reason, I believe God began to place me in circles with people who had the "stick-to-itiveness" I needed to pursue my destiny. Not that my current friends were not go-getters, but God knew that for me to do a new thing, He had to show me an example of a new thing. I began to attend conferences and join organizations where I was influenced by game changers. I associated myself with problem solvers and chain breakers. These people would help to influence and change the way I pursued the dreams, goals, and visions God gave to me. They challenged me to reach beyond my ability and tap into a strength I didn't know I possessed.

Let's think about it this way. Remember pressure cookers? My mom used her pressure cooker to make cabbage, greens, soups, etc. Pressure cookers work by utilizing built up steam from boiling food inside the pot to cook. Once the pot reaches maximum pressure, the heat can be decreased, and the food will continue to cook based on the internal temperature the steam created in the pot.

Developing a strong work ethic works similarly to a pressure cooker. By having the stick-to-itiveness to keep moving toward destiny, we are developing what is needed to push through times when we don't feel like our purpose is taking us anywhere. Our internal pressure cooker or work ethic keeps us moving when we don't feel like working. When we feel like giving up and throwing in the towel, we can turn up the heat (i.e. work ethic) and keep moving.

There is more to work ethic than working when we do not feel like it. An important component to developing a quality work ethic is remembering who and why it is you are doing the work. If we think about pursuing our purpose to earn money, what happens when the money doesn't come in? If we pursue our purpose to gain attention, popularity, or favor with man, what if we never receive the praise we were hoping for? Walking in purpose in the path of destiny must be done unto God. He is the only person who will give us the satisfaction, gratification, and fulfillment we are searching for in this journey. Pursuing goals to gain satisfaction from things or people that are not guaranteed will only leave us hopeless if we do not receive from them what we are desire.

Another important component to developing our work ethic/stick-to-itiveness is getting free from distractions. Distractions are set up to knock us off course. They present themselves innocently and harmless, but distractions detour us away from our goals. We must be aware of what poses a distraction in our life. For some of us, a distraction may be social media, having certain conversations with friends, or the simple thoughts swirling around in our heads. To stay focused on our destiny, we must be aware of what causes us to be distracted. We have to figure out what prohibits us from working toward the goal God has set before us. For me, it was fear. I was afraid I wasn't going to be good enough. I was afraid I would not succeed. So, I chose to take the comfortable route. Instead of doing what God told me to do, I did what was safe. Allowing myself to become distracted (and crippled) by fear, I allowed myself to become distracted by thoughts that were not real. My distraction was in the form of what I allowed myself to think and believe. It wasn't until I was fed up that I decided it was time to move beyond the distractions and focus instead on what God had already told me that I could start moving toward my destiny.

Work ethic and stick-to-itiveness are not the only tools we need to move in the direction of our destiny. Desire is a major component of our destiny.

Desire is defined as the want or wish for something; the longing or hope for something. When we desire something, our heart sends signals to our brain about what we are envisioning. Desire is an absolute necessary component of our destiny. If we do not desire to walk in our destiny, we have no desire to pursue our purpose or obey the Word of God. Thus, we are ultimately refusing to live the best life we could possibly live. Our desire comes down to what is in our heart. We must ask ourselves, "What does my heart crave? What is my heart telling me?"

If we are in a position where we do not know what our desire is, we must go to the source of our desires - God. Psalm 37 teaches us that when we commit ourselves to God, He will give us the desires of our heart. The first step in understanding what we desire is giving our complete self to God and asking Him to reveal to us what is deep down in our hearts. After all, we are created in the image of Him. We are a manifestation of His desire.

The question for some may not be, "What do I desire?" but rather, "How do I take my desire and spring it into action toward my destiny?" The answer is fire. For a fire to burn, there must be oxygen and fuel. If destiny is our fire, purpose and desire are the fuel needed for it to burn. We have to combine our destiny and purpose to create movement towards destiny. Combining desire with purpose creates the perfect fire for our destiny. When we can pinpoint our purpose and channel our desire (what our heart is envisioning), then we can take action steps i.e. creating business plans, going back to school, starting a non-profit, or whatever is necessary to achieve our destiny.

The last, but still equally important, component of destiny is patience. I'm not the most patient person, but I am learning. Growing up, I had a poster on my door that read, "Patience is a virtue. Seek it and enjoy its riches". I'm not sure why, but out of all the quotes on the poster, my eyes always gravitated toward this one.

We live in a microwave generation. Everyone wants everything now, except God. He understands the beauty in patience. Patience creates an atmosphere for growth, cultivation, maturation, and many other things needed to walk in the fullness of our destiny. I often ask my friends, "If God gave us everything we wanted right now at this moment, would we be ready to receive it all?" Many times, the answer is no. God understands the importance of building and growing from place to place. If we were given everything we wanted, chances are we would mess it up. Plans would not flow correctly, goals would not be achieved in excellence, and business plans would not garner the support or funding needed.

Destiny requires us to walk in patience. As we experience new things and God introduces to new aspects of our purpose, we need to take the time necessary to learn and process how each piece is beneficial to our destiny. We must take the time to process the weightiness each moment plays on our destiny. If we miss the moment, we are bound to repeat the lesson until we truly grasp what God is trying to teach us.

Only in patience can we understand the beauty in God's timing and allow experience to cultivate our future. The book of Genesis teaches about seed, time, and harvest. God tells us that as long as the earth remains, there will always be seed, time, and harvest. The reason for this is that God wants to create an understanding of patience. When we are patient, all great things happen at the right time. If we impatiently move ahead of time, chances are the harvest will not be the best it could possibly be. We could potentially kill the seed we planted, thus ruining the harvest. Our destiny operates the same way.

If we are impatient and choose to move too quickly, we have the potential to thwart our destiny. The very last thing anyone should hope for is a damaged and delayed destiny.

Destiny Steps

Ask Yourself…
- Do I have a healthy work ethic?
- What does my heart desire?
- Am I walking in patience while God works out my destiny piece by piece?

YOUR DESTINY MOMENT

Often, we are in such a rush to pursue projects or completed goals. Take time before implementing your goals to ask yourself, "Why is this goal so important to me? Who am I doing this for? What do I hope to accomplish or achieve?" After you have answered these questions, be sure to pinpoint any distractions that could hinder your progress.

Chapter Six

Fireproof

My Destiny Steps: *Courageous. Fearful. Determined*

After 35 years, if I could use one word to describe myself it would be safe. I've never really been a risk taker nor would I describe myself as adventurous. I tend to choose activities or jobs that allow a certain level of comfort. I normally never choose to do anything that would have me to step too far outside of the box. However, if there is one thing I have learned since moving to Atlanta, it's the importance of being brave. Quitting my job and moving over 700 miles away from my friends and family took a certain level of bravado that I did not think I had. I've always been independent, but brave – not so much. Caution was always my rule of thumb, but I reached a point where I could no longer take the safe route. I could only take the route that led me to my destiny. Living life on the safe side excluded me from God's power. Choosing to be safe instead of stepping out on faith was me inadvertently telling God, " Hey, God. I don't really want to do things Your way. I'm ok over here. " I was content with living a "just enough" life. God hasn't called us to live a "just enough" life. He wants us to live an abundant life. Trying to do what is safe limits God's power, His hand, and desire to lead us into our destiny.

Destiny requires us to be brave. It requires us to stand up to what frightens us the most. Fear has been one thing that has crippled me from walking in my destiny. What I've learned is that the more I continue to move forward, the more the fear dissipates, and the stronger my determination grows. If we are to be courageous, fear cannot be what holds us back. Fear is essentially the opposite of faith. If we are choosing to hide behind our fears and not take our destiny by the horns, we are letting fear win. But if we want to be kings and queens and take what God has already told us is ours, we must take it and do so with boldness and tenacity. I once heard this example: The jaws of a bulldog are specifically designed in such a way that anything placed in their mouth cannot be pulled away easily. They have a larger jaw and shorter nose area making it easier to take hold of something and not let it go. This is the same way we should be when it comes to our destiny. We should be bold and tenacious. We should take our purpose, lock it in the jaws of our spirit, and refuse to let it go. We cannot allow fear or worry to come in and snatch away from us what God has already placed within our grasp.

What do we do when fear seems unbearable or when we are lacking the determination and boldness to press forward and grab hold of our destiny? When fear seems unbearable and we are lacking determination, we must fight through those emotions. It is important to push ourselves, speak to our fear, and build ourselves according to the Word of God. We must remember everything He has already told us and remind ourselves that God has a plan and purpose to prosper us. We must remind ourselves that we were born for a time such as this. We must remind ourselves that we were birthed to be the answer to a problem.

Whether we think we are strong or not, we have to understand that strength is not found in our own ability. There will be times when life is happening around us, and we just don't have the fortitude to keep going. That's when we have to turn everything over to God. God reassures us that He is the one who can and will lift our heads when we are unable to (Psalm 3:3 NLT).

We don't have to do things in our own strength. While God has called us to be strong, we have to realize the ability to push through is found in Him. There will be times in our pursuit of destiny when we will feel weak. Our strength will be at its lowest. In these moments, we have to fight against our weaknesses and push forward. When King David was a teenager, he was anointed to be King of Israel, but had to endure a series of tasks, tests, and trials before taking the throne. The most infamous task was defeating Goliath the Philistine. Goliath was a colossal giant compared to David. When everyone else feared Goliath, David stepped in to take him down. He channeled the strength God anointed him with and managed to kill Goliath. Destiny is the giant in many of our lives. It seems too strong to conquer and beyond our grasp, but that isn't the case. God has already provided us with what we need to pursue purpose and walk in destiny. We have to choose to be courageous and fear not what is in front of us.

Destiny Steps

Ask Yourself…

- What am I afraid of?
- Does my determination outweigh my desire to live life on the "safe route"?

YOUR DESTINY MOMENT

For some of us, fear is very real. It is crippling and has altered our life. Isaiah 54:4 tells us to "fear not." What is the cause of your fear? Is it failure, past mistakes, or not living up to a certain standard? In the face of fear, we have to choose faith. We cannot let fear hinder us from achieving goals and living out the dreams God has placed in our hearts. Above all else, when we are facing fear head on, we have to be courageous and bold. Decide that today will be the day you will step forward and kick fear in the face!

Chapter Seven
Checks and Balances

My Destiny Moment: *People. Are. Essential*

I like to consider myself an introverted extrovert. I love people, but I also love my personal space and quiet time. Growing up, I was the shy child who never wanted to speak in public. I've always found more comfort in solitude than in large groups of people. When alone, I can think, clear my mind, dream, and visualize. Being an introvert allows me to connect with who I am. It is in this peaceful place that I am most comfortable being who I am. I can be awkward, silly, a singer, or anything else I feel I cannot be among others. This is also my safe place. I do not have to worry about other people's opinions of me. I do not have to think about if I am being judged. I do not have to deal with being misunderstood. I am completely free to be exactly who I am. The downside of this is the potential to exclude other people.

Being an introvert comes with inadvertently separating ourselves from other people. We are so comfortable in our little space that we only make room for those who have proven they deserve a space. We only confide information to certain people who have earned the right to join us in our solitude. The problem with this mentality is that God did not design life to be this way. No man is an island. We cannot do life with only ourselves nor can we choose to coexist with only a few select people. We are all on this earth collectively, and whether we like it or not, we need people. People are essential to our growth, maturity, and destiny.

It was not until I was alone in a new city that I realized the importance of people. It took complete solitude and isolation for me to realize the importance of each person I had encountered. Doing life with people has the innate ability to show you exactly who you are. Whether you realize it or not, the people in our lives operate much like a mirror. They reflect who we are rather than who we think we are.

I can remember attending a conference and hearing a simple, yet profound comment. The speaker said, "We are the sum of the five closest people in our circle." After hearing this, I had to re-evaluate who was closest to me, and if the sum of who we are collectively were characteristics I desired to have. Ironically, I did not have anyone in my inner circle at the time. I had completely removed myself from my inner circle, thus leaving me with only myself to compare my life. However, I had God on the inside of me telling me I needed people.

God constantly reminded me I needed interaction with other people to move into my destiny. I could not retreat inside of my comfortable turtle shell and hide from the world while trying to discover my purpose. God reminded me that people are essential to my destiny and my purpose. People are necessary components of my growth and maturity. Without impact, influence, and interaction with people, I was doomed to fail.

To understand just how imperative people are to my destiny, I asked myself what, "What have you learned from other people? The answer was simple. I still had a lot more growing and maturing to do before I could reach my destiny. Because people can act as a mirror in our lives, they can see what we think we are hiding. They can see through the selfishness and toddler-like personality traits. People have the ability to challenge those areas we are afraid to tap into. They can see who we are afraid to become or the issues that hinder us from becoming all that God has called us to be. The people in our lives are designed to shed light on the areas we are darkest. Once the light has been shined, we can begin the process of growing and maturing as needed to reach our destiny.

The people in our lives act as a proverbial checks and balances systems in our lives. The checks and balances system was designed to "check" each branch of the federal government ensuring power is "balanced" across the board. The people in our lives operate the same way. They serve as a "check" to be sure our lives are in order. Many times, my friends have come together to let me know what I need to work on. Whether it be my attitude or professional goals, the people I surround myself with make sure I'm living a life that is in order and on track.

We cannot rely solely on the people closest to us to operate as a check system. There must also be balance. The people in our life should level us out, make sure we are well-rounded, and ensure that there is not too much of one thing going on in our lives. As I said earlier, I am an introvert. I'm also a classic Type A personality. I like things to be done efficiently, effectively, and with a razor-like focus. Having a personality such as this often means I lack a life of complete balance. I view a lot of things as either black or white, leaving little room for gray areas. When I'm working, I tap into that razor-like focus. I am very adept at shutting out my surroundings to focus on my work. Sometimes, this means I rarely come up for air when I'm focused. That's where balance comes into play. The people in my life are there to bring me out of my tent so I can get some air. They help bring understanding and a certain level of softness to my otherwise harsh, black and white thinking.

We often hear the term opposites attract. Why do opposites attract? Why do two elements with nothing in common seem to mesh so well together? Think about peanut butter and apples. Why is this such a delicious combination? One is sweet (or sour depending on the apple) with a mild flavor and a slight crunch, and the other smooth with a very robust flavor. Though they are very different, these two flavors and textures collided make the perfect snack! People who are opposite from us create the same balance. Where we are weak, they are strong. They have an abundance of the area we lack. Where we are void of understanding, they can create space in our minds for reason.

We cannot live life without balance or the people who create balance. God has crafted them with the ability to maintain the juxtaposition of our lives. There are times when destiny will require us to perform balancing acts. We will be required to balance relationships, work, children, etc. Certain people are placed in our lives to provide balance. They are there to remind us when we need a time out, when we need to refocus on Christ, and when we need to realign our priorities. Without balance, we are setting ourselves up for a life of over commitment, confusion, and burnout. To be in the best space for our destiny, we need to live a completely balanced life.

The connections and relationships I have with people are helping to shape the way I grow and mature into my destiny. If I encircle myself with the right connections, I can be sure I will be on the right path to destiny. On the contrary, having the wrong connections have the potential to cause me to regress and fall backward away from my destiny. It is imperative that we discern right connections from wrong connections. The best way to decide if a connection is beneficial is to look at them as depreciating or appreciating. For this to make better sense, think of this in terms of the value of a car. The moment a brand-new car leaves the car lot, it automatically depreciates or loses value – sometimes up to $10K. Whereas a home for example, the longer you own it, the more its value increases or appreciates. Our connections work in the same way. They either add value to your life or take away from it.

It's imperative that we are aware of the value our chosen connections play in our life. They have the ability to bring us beneficial opportunities that propel us further into our destiny or cause us to backslide out of the path of destiny. According to Luke 6:38, God uses men to provide us with the opportunities we need. God is the source and man is the resource. Our connections are the vehicle God uses to bless us.

Who we are connected to not only plays an important role in our growth and maturity, but it also plays a major role in holding us accountable. Accountability is key when on a specific path toward destiny. Those who we are accountable to are the same ones authorized to "check and balance" our life. We should be accountable to someone. There should always be a person or group of people who at any given moment can probe us to be sure we are on the correct path. In the event we have fallen off course, those same people should be able to provide us with the necessary guidance that will get us back on track. I rely on my personal group of girlfriends to keep me in line when it comes to my destiny. I rely on their honesty and guidance to keep me on track. They are especially helpful when I have fallen off the grid. My girlfriends are much more than just people I am connected to, they are my accountability. If I want to make a decision or if I am struggling with a specific issue, I know I can always go to them. They will not say what I want to hear, but rather what I need to hear. The people we are accountable to are not our "yes" men and women. They are individuals with whom we are in covenant. After God, we trust them to keep our lives in order.

Destiny is not all about us. The people around us play a crucial role in who we are becoming. We must recognize that our destiny will not be everything God desires it to be if we continue to live a life that devalues the importance of people. We should see the value other people play in our lives if we want to live a life that is destiny-centered.

Destiny Steps

Ask Yourself...

- Who am I connected to?
- Do I have beneficial connections?
- Do I view the people in my life as "right" or "wrong" connections?
- Are the people in my life continuing to push me along a path of growth and maturity?

YOUR DESTINY MOMENT

Do not be afraid to analyze the circle of people in your life. Because someone has been an essential component of your life in the past does not automatically guarantee him or her a seat in your destiny. How do the people in your life influence you? How are you influencing them? Are the people in your life appreciating or depreciating your worth? Take some time to evaluate the role people play in your life. Determine if these people are holding you accountable to your destiny or holding you back and causing you to live a life stuck in the past.

Chapter Eight
Through the Looking Glass

My Destiny Moment: *You don't have all the answers!*

Mirror, Mirror on the wall, please tell me people don't think I'm a "know-it-all." We hear all the time how no one likes a "know-it-all." Unfortunately, I must confess that sometimes I can be a "know-it-all." As I continue my journey to destiny, I have learned that I tend to think I have all the answers. That's hard to admit. One of the toughest lessons I've learned over the past few years is that I am not as smart or as wise as I think I am. There will always be someone with more experience and/or more wisdom than I have, and that's okay. It's actually a good thing.

Growing into the person God desires me to be comes with a few pains. One of those pains was learning that I do not have all the answers and I am not the wisest. Often, this lesson shows up when I work with other people. Working with others can sometimes be challenging for me because I want to do things my way. I had to (and still have to) learn that my way is not always the best way. I may not always have all of the necessary experience to complete every task.

My maturation process has continuously shown me that wisdom is an essential component to my destiny. The insight and experience locked inside the minds of other people will help lead and guide me into the direction God desires me to go. A few years ago, my dad decided to become a franchise owner. He transitioned from Corporate America into entrepreneurship. While he had always ran small businesses along with his corporate job, operating a franchise was something entirely new. For him to be successful, he had to spend time and glean from those who had been in the business much longer and had acquired more experience. If he decided to become a franchise owner and forego the wisdom of more experienced owners/operators he would do himself a disservice. Ignoring the wisdom and experience of others is committing the ultimate disservice to our destiny.

Wisdom is the key that helps to unlock our destiny. If we do not have the instructions on how to reach our destiny, we will never get there. Wisdom says I have been there, I have done that, and I have the experience and lessons needed to carry you into the next phase of your destiny. God understands this, which is why he tells us in Hosea 4:6 that we are destroyed for our lack of knowledge. God understands the importance of wisdom. Not just wisdom from any source, but wisdom from sources that have stood the test of time (experience).

When we choose to dismiss the importance of wisdom, we begin to step into pride. Pride says we have all the answers and do not need the expertise of others. According to Proverbs 16, pride comes before our fall. Stepping into pride is the beginning of our demise. There is nothing in God's plan for our destiny that says we must fail. Believing we do not need guidance and wisdom opens the door for failure. Believing we are smarter, wiser, better, and more important than those who have the experience we need, solidifies our impending failure. We cannot afford to fail because of our prideful heart and lack of wisdom.

How do we embrace wisdom and prevent our hearts from being filled with pride? The first step is transparency. I've mentioned before the importance of transparency, and I will mention it here again because of the weight it carries. I have to be honest and admit that transparency used to be a struggle for me. I struggled with transparency partly because I didn't know myself well enough to be transparent and partly because my heart was filled with pride. In my mind, transparency equated to needing others. I refrained from transparency because I didn't want the input of others. I was afraid that someone would tell me what was wrong with my mindset, feelings, and systems of operation – PRIDE! It took time, openness, and vulnerability for me to become comfortable with being transparent. I had to understand that transparency allowed God to work certain things in me and break things off me that were hindrances to my destiny.

We have to view transparency the same way. God only wants to pour into us those things that will propel us into destiny. If we cannot be open about our struggles and what we lack, how can we expect God to get to us what we need? There are people in our social and professional circles willing to help us get to the next phase of our destiny. Refusing to be vulnerable limits the assistance those circles can provide us. Many people assume vulnerability is a weakness, but it is not. Exposing our vulnerability eliminates a haughty and prideful heart. Vulnerability says I do not have all the answers, and I need help. Being vulnerable breaks the chains of pride in our hearts and creates a blank canvas in our hearts for wisdom and guidance to take root.

We cannot move into destiny if we refuse to admit the areas we are the most insecure. Most people view insecurities as a weakness because they are afraid others will prey upon their weakness and take advantage of them. Much like admitting the areas we are most vulnerable, admitting where we are the most insecure allows growth to occur. If we are afraid of our insecurities, we are afraid to grow. Acknowledging our insecure areas creates a platform for God to come in and establish total dependence on Him that cannot be found in people, places or things.

One of the most important keys to creating an environment conducive to openness, removing insecurities, and eliminating vulnerability is allowing ourselves to be corrected and rebuked. Correction shows us what we are doing wrong in hopes that we turn away from the error. Destiny demands rebuke and correction to take place to ensure our behavior is aligned properly with the purpose and vision God has for our lives. Refusing to be corrected and/or rebuked opens the door to pride. A prideful heart is an enemy of wisdom and a hindrance to our destiny. However, for correction and rebuke to be effective and used as a proper learning tool, they must come from trusted sources. Not everyone is privy to the intimacy needed to give accurate rebuke and correction. Those who have journeyed with us through life and have proven to be trusted voices are granted the ability to correct and rebuke attitudes, mentalities, and behaviors that are damaging to our destiny.

Think about the number of times our parents or teachers challenged our behavior. I can confess to being checked numerous times about my behavior. At the time, I felt like my parents were being unfair. I now know that they were doing so from a place of love. People who care, love you, and want to see you walk in the fullness of your destiny will correct and/or rebuke you from a place of love. When love is the motivation for the correction, we should be receptive and willing to take corrective action.

Destiny Steps

Ask Yourself…

- Who is my wise counsel?
- Who can I trust to provide the wisdom and guidance I need for my destiny?
- Am I open to correction and rebuke?
- Am I too prideful to admit the areas I am weakest in and need the most help?

Your Destiny Steps

Think about the importance wisdom plays in your destiny. Proverbs 12:1 tells us that in order to learn, we must love discipline and that it is stupid to hate correction. How many times have we refused to be corrected because we only want to be right or we think we have all the answers? Our unwillingness is only leading us down a prideful path away from knowledge. What steps can you take today to open yourself up to wisdom and knowledge from unlikely sources? What can you do to prevent yourself from shying away from the expertise found in the minds of others who have done the work before you? Commit to being wise and gleaning from the wisdom of others. Choose to see vulnerabilities, not as a weakness, but rather a stepping stone to strength. Learn to be content with admitting your insecurities and allowing God to be your strength.

Chapter Nine

Fingerprints

My Destiny Moment: *Unity. Connectedness. Uniquely You.*

I grew up playing basketball and volleyball. Basketball was and still is my favorite sport. I remember watching the inaugural season on the WNBA in June 1997. My love for team sports grew as I secured a spot on my high school's basketball team. If there is one thing I learned playing basketball, in addition to teamwork, it would be uniqueness. We all know it takes a team to win games and championships, but during teamwork and unity, there are unique talents and gifts found in each player and coach. One of my favorite basketball coaches to date is Larry Brown. In my eyes, Coach Larry Brown has the unique and sometimes innate ability to mesh together multiple personalities on a team to remain focused on a common goal – winning. I watched as he coached the Philadelphia 76ers and Allen Iverson and also as he led the Detroit Pistons to their 2004 NBA Finals Championship. Both of those teams consisted of multiple highly talented players with unique skills and abilities. To me, Larry Brown could decipher and decode each skill, allowing them to be used at the most strategic and opportune time during the game.

Our destiny does not operate much different than the game of basketball or any other team sport. Amid pursuing our destiny, there are unique qualities that God will begin to reveal in us as needed. Sometimes, our unique skills and abilities come across as awkward leaving us with feelings of being an outcast. When God places certain quirks and personality traits in the midst of our genetic makeup, it is not meant to seclude us from everyone else or what we deem as "normal." God's intended plan is for us to discover just how unique we are as individuals. It's our identity. It's who we are. Many of us cannot welcome specific qualities about ourselves because we do not know who we are. We have yet to identify ourselves.

If I'm reviewing specific features of a car belonging to a Tesla and want to know what makes it different from a Mercedes, I'm not going to visit the Land Rover dealer. I'm going to visit the one who can identify the make, model, and year of the vehicle. If we cannot identify who we are, we cannot identify our purpose and began the route to destiny. The only way we can identify who we are is to consult with our Maker.

Think about our fingerprints. They are our very own unique identifier. No one has or will ever share the same fingerprints. Identical twins share the same DNA and physical features, but each are born with a unique set of fingerprints. God is so intentional in creation that He births two babies from one egg with two separate sets of fingerprints to be sure they understand just how unique they truly are! We should approach our destiny in the same manner. We may have similar gifts, but the uniqueness found in our personalities is what makes us special.

Embracing what is different and/or unique is often the challenge. What we see as different and unusual, God sees as beautiful. Psalm 139:14 proves this by describing each person on this earth as fearfully and wonderfully made. God created each person on this earth out of a desire He had in His heart. In all our differences and beauty, God sees us as wonderful creations formed out of His image. We are different in various ways, but God saw fit to create each and every one of us. In all our differences we find the glory of God.

It can be hard to love what is different, especially if we do not understand the importance of why something is different. I am a firm believer that people are born with different challenges to show the world the beauty in everything. In 1 Corinthians 12, the Apostle Paul teaches us about the human body in relation to spiritual gifts. It is in this scripture that we see the importance in being different. Although we have different and unique functions in the body of

Christ, each one is just as effective and needed as the next.

Our destiny requires us to tap into and discover what makes us unique. As I have become comfortable with what makes me unique, I've watched as my differences attract specific and unlikely people to my journey. Some of the friends I have now I may never have associated with because they are so different from who I am. What makes us different are qualities I never knew I desired or needed. I am now able to uncover just how much I needed their individuality in my life to achieve a life of duality and purpose. In our differences, we have found unity, friendship and the will to push one another toward our destiny.

There are times in the midst of discovering just how beautiful our differences can be that we view those differences as competition. I can recall many times in my life (even now) watching as friends and associates pursued their dynamic callings from God. Instead of being supportive and encouraging, I developed feelings of competition and envy. I didn't want to support them. I wanted to be better than them. I wanted to achieve more just so I could say that I have done more and moved further along in my purpose and destiny. I had to have a "come to Jesus" talk with myself. I had to have a serious sit down with God and ask why I was feeling the way I felt. His answer was simple, sweet, gentle, and to the point – it was because I didn't know who I was. Since I didn't know who I was, I could not support others or welcome the way in which they pursued their destiny. Because I did not know who God called me to be or how He was going to execute His calling on my life, I chose to view others as competition. I lacked the understanding that all things work together for the good of those who love God and are called according to His purpose.

My misunderstanding of purpose and ignorance to how God was going to use all those who believe in Him collectively to make His name great caused a rift in my interaction with others. I viewed everyone as competition. I could not see the beauty in our different purposes and how effectively we operated in the areas God had called us to.

Everyone was competition. I had to beat out everyone else. I quickly learned that I was only beating myself. I put myself in a perpetual trick bag of sorts thinking if I did better than someone else, I must have more anointing or a higher calling. None of my thinking was even close to being the truth.

Instead of viewing one another as competition, we should see one another as learning opportunities. The people in our lives who are stronger in certain areas can teach us and make us strong where we are weak. Paul proves this in Galatians 6 as he admonishes us to carry the weight of others. We need others who are already strong in certain areas to bring us up to the level we need to be. Likewise, those who are strongest should not view those who are weak as a burden, but as opportunity to grow themselves and strengthen their brothers and sisters in Christ.

When we view one another as teammates instead of opponents, we can accomplish our destiny steps quicker and more efficiently. Remember, we are like fingerprints – everyone has them, but they are all different and unique.

Destiny Steps

Ask Yourself…

- Do I view my peers as teammates or as opponents?
- Do I understand the unique qualities that exist with me?
- Am I committed to pursuing my destiny and purpose under the guise of unity and connectedness?

YOUR DESTINY MOMENT

God is our potter and we are His clay. Each one of us has been molded and shaped according the area God desires to place us. Embrace what makes you different. If you do not know, ask God. Ask Him to reveal the special qualities He has created within you. Once you have done this, take the time to discover how you can be part of Team Jesus as we make Him famous. Remember, you are fearfully and wonderfully made. There is no manufacturers defect inside of you. God created you specifically with a destiny and goal in mind. Uncover what makes you unique and celebrate with those around you as you walk into your destiny.

Chapter Ten

The Three Little P's

My Destiny Moment: *Plan. Prepare. Process.*

One of my favorite fairytale stories growing up was "The Three Little Pigs." In this story, there were three little pigs. Each had their own fortune to build a house. The first pig chose to build a house made of straw. The second chose to build a house made of sticks. The third pig chose to build a house made of bricks.

I will continue with a synopsis of the story, but this initial piece of the fairytale speaks to the importance of process. Each pig had to go through a unique process to reach his goal. Within my journey to destiny, I had to go through a process. There were a series of steps. The first was saying yes to the process. Committing to the process meant I agreed to the procedure necessary to reach my destiny. Many times, we want to reach our goal, but deny the process. We want to see our dream materialize, but ignore the steps needed to see them become a reality.

The Three Little Pigs grasped the importance of process. They understood that for them to reach their destiny, a new house, they had to take specific action steps. Each step depended on the accuracy of the previous step. Assuming these three pigs were highly intelligent, (I mean how many pigs do you know with the capability to build homes?) they must have understood that part of the process included exposure. Let's assume this was the first time each pig had ever built a house. As they laid the foundation for their homes, they began to learn through the building process what they were truly made of. They began to learn new skill sets. They began to learn what it meant to endure. They began to learn what it meant to be tenacious. How many of us can say that while in the midst of purpose and building our destiny, we have submitted ourselves to the process and the exposure that comes along with it? How many of us are willing to surrender to being exposed and pulled apart to reveal what is really living on the inside of us? The process is not only about the steps we take to reach our destiny, but also what we allow God to pull in and out of us.

During the beginning stages of my destiny process, God began to expose my true character. He began to expose my desire to serve as well as my selfish tendencies. He began to show me that I had everything I needed to accomplish my destiny, but that I was lazy in the pursuit of my purpose. He also showed me what steps I needed to take to ensure a successful traveling path to my destiny. I had to let go of unfruitful relationships, speak life over myself, and say YES to the process. God cannot and will not do anything in us without our yes.

While the process is an important component to destiny, it is not the only component. Prior to building their homes, the three little pigs must have had a plan in place. There must have been a blueprint for how they were going to build their house. The pigs must have known that to be successful, they needed a strategy. Our destiny operates in the same manner. If we are going to succeed in purpose and move into our destiny, we cannot forsake planning. Benjamin Franklin once said, "If you fail to plan, you are planning to fail."

It is important that we understand the importance of planning. God operates in decency and order (1 Corinthians 14:40). The only way we can align ourselves with this teaching is if we have a plan. When I made the decision to pick up my life and move to Atlanta, I didn't have every detail secured, but I dId have a plan. Because I did not have any family in Georgia, I had to study the area where I wanted to move. I had to communicate with property managers. I had to create a roadmap for my new life. On the contrary, my plans were limited because all I knew was God said, "Now is the time to relocate to Atlanta." In the moments where we do not have a plan, but we but we have a word from God, we need to consult Him. We need to spend time before God so He can download His plans and instruction into our hearts and mind.

Even if we do have a plan, it is imperative that we commune with God to be sure what we have planned is indicative of the plan He has for our lives. We have to trust the plan and vision God has for our lives. Trusting the plan and vision He has for us starts with acknowledging that although we cannot see the end result of where God is taking us, the path we are on is evidence that God is strategizing on behalf of our destiny. Submitting to God's plans is an act of faith. God's ways are higher than our ways, and His thoughts are higher than our thoughts. As the Author of our lives, God knows what is best for our destiny. God has already created plans, roadmaps, strategies for us to follow to ensure a successful transition into our destiny. If we try to figure out the plan for our lives without consulting the Creator, we are asking for a difficult journey. Even worse, we are asking for a delayed destiny.

One of the gateways to our destiny is not only planning and processing but also preparation. When careful preparation meets the right opportunity, we are destined for success. While we cannot deem the time when opportunity will manifest, we can prepare to receive it.

In the fairytale, only one of the three little pigs understood the importance of careful preparation.

Out of the three, he was the only one aware of the wolf scoping the scene waiting to attack. He knew there was going to be an opportunity for the wolf to attack him and his brothers. To successfully build a home to withstand the wolf's attack, he had to be prepared.

The third pig also understood the weight of what could happen if he did not prepare. Luke 14:28 necessitates that we count the cost of what we choose to embark upon. While we cannot anticipate hardships or bumps in the road, we can create a plan and a process that will prepare us for what may lie ahead. We should consider the heaviness of what we are preparing for. We must think about the people we will encounter, the lives that will be changed, how our lives will be impacted, and how God will be glorified. There is a weight that comes with everyone's assignment. Abraham, Noah, and even Jesus all carried the weight of what their destiny required. In the weightiness, they understood the importance of being prepared.

Preparation also requires us to make ourselves ready for something we expect to happen. If we expect to walk into our destiny, then we must ready ourselves for the moment destiny presents itself.

We cannot ready ourselves if we are not prepared. If we do not have an in-depth understanding of what our destiny entails, there is no way we can effectively prepare for it. Part of what our destiny entails is people who doubt and may question our actions. Everyone will not understand why we do what we do for the sake of destiny. There are people who do not believe they have a purpose and destiny. There are people who simply do not believe in destiny at all. Because of those people, we have to be secure in Christ and the direction He is taking us. There should be no room for people to doubt and question the instructions God has given us.

I can remember a number of times people questioned my decision to move to Atlanta. People did not understand why I would quit a perfectly good job and move 700 miles away to a city where I had no family or job – but I understood. My understanding of how God was maneuvering through my life kept the doubt at a minimum. There were times I questioned God about what He was doing, but His peace quickly reassured me that all was well and I was on the right path. We cannot allow the doubt of others to hinder the destiny steps we are taking. Doubt leads to distractions and distractions lead us down the wrong path. We must remain focused on God and secure in how He is leading us. We have to learn to be bold by declaring that there is nothing we will not do to follow the steps God has ordered for us.

Process, Planning, and Preparation (The Three Little P's) are essential components to our destiny. Like the Three Little Pigs, we have to undergo a process, create a plan for how we will flourish in our destiny, and ensure we have undergone sufficient preparation. Following through with these three things will help us successfully transition into destiny.

Destiny Steps

Ask Yourself…

- Am I adequately prepared for my purpose and destiny?
- Am I choosing to go through the necessary process in order to walk in my destiny?
- What can I do to better prepare myself?
- Have I allowed God to download his plan into my heart?

YOUR DESTINY MOMENT

PLAN, PREPARE, and PROCESS are essential to our destiny. We must understand that there are strategic steps God has ordered us to take to ensure our success. God does not want us to fail, nor should we expect to fail. Destiny is ultimately a marathon race we will win if we take the time to prepare ourselves, go through the process, and proceed with a plan. Allow God to show you His plan. Be content and satisfied with the plan God has for you knowing it is greater than anything you could have ever anticipated. Position your heart to follow through with God's plan knowing your destiny is on the other side.

Chapter Eleven

All Hail the Victors!

My Destiny Moment: *You're more than a conqueror.*
You are victorious!

The year was 1991. I was in the 5th grade. My teacher's name was Mrs. Johnson. We were playing an intense spelling game. I had made it to the final round, and only one opponent stood in the way of my victory. I knew I was going to win. The word we had to spell was salmon. It was a tricky word because the 'L' is silent. My dad had taught me how to spell 'salmon' correctly just prior to our spelling game. My opponent went first. I listened intently as she forgot the letter 'L". I knew I had won. Finally, it was my turn, and I spelled it correctly. I was the champion!! If a song could have been playing in my head, it would have been the song by Queen, *"We are the champions my friend, and we'll keep on fighting 'til the end...no time for losers because we are the champions of the world!"*

I've always been quite competitive. I'm not sure where it comes from. Maybe it is because I am the oldest. I'm not sure, but my level of competitiveness is pretty high. I want to be victorious. I enjoy winning. My destiny...your destiny...our destiny is predicated on us being victorious. Victory doesn't happen overnight. It starts as a mindset. We must declare first that we are victors if we truly want to be victorious. We cannot march on into destiny or fight the battle of purposelessness if we continuously believe we are losers. According to Proverbs 23:7, we are who we believe we are in our hearts. How we think about ourselves determines how we will end up. It is important that we plant seeds of victory in our hearts. We have to think about the good things of God. We have to meditate on His promises to ensure we walk victoriously into our destiny. We don't want to stumble into our purpose, we want to command it and demand God to reveal it to us.

Our destiny requires that we think on those things that are honest, just, pure, lovely, and of good report. Thinking of these things will keep us on track to our destiny. When thoughts try to creep in and persuade us that we are not victors, we have to take those thoughts captive and surrender them to Christ. We must stay hungry and thirsty for our destiny and victory. We must be so fierce that the same enemy that preys upon us like a roaring lion, cowards away from us because he knows he is facing a losing battle. We have the King of Glory on our side, therefore, we are strong and mighty in battle. This is what makes us victorious. This is what gives us the ability to conquer anything that tries to set itself up against us and take our crown.

Reminding ourselves that we are victors is only one piece of the puzzle. We have to be reminded that we are also overcomers. Being an overcomer says I have fought a hard battle, but I am not defeated. Being victorious in pursuit of destiny means we are not willing to give up. It means that we will continue to fight the good fight because we believe in the promises God has laid out before us. There will be trials and hard times as long as we are on the earth, but we have been given the power and ability in Jesus to overcome. Part of being an overcomer means we must endure. I can recall many moments when I had to keep going no matter how much I wanted to throw in the towel. It's not fun nor is it enjoyable, but there is victory on the other side.

After about three years of living in Atlanta, I had a conversation with God. I asked Him why He allowed me to move if I wasn't going to make major strides in my purpose. Why did He have me in this city with no family and none of my close friends if I wasn't going make major career moves? God began to show me that being in Atlanta was not about the actual work, but more importantly my endurance to keep fighting. By enduring and continuing to persevere, we show God that we want what it is He has for us. If we can endure and persevere, we have what it takes to keep standing and walking into destiny.

The pursuit of destiny is not easy. There will be walls God has to tear down before He can erect something new in our life. We have to be free from our past. We have to let go of the old and embrace the new. We have to renew our minds according to the vision God has placed before us. We have to remain in expectation and full of hope. Even though the vision and our destiny may tarry, we must keep pushing. Even though it may seem as if God is taking forever to deliver on His promises, we have to remain hopeful. When it is all said and done, when we have learned the lesson, when we have fought and made it to the land of milk and honey, then and only then will we discover that destiny has been fulfilled. It won't come overnight. It won't happen if we don't desire it to happen. Destiny won't manifest if we refuse to move and get into the place and position in which God has called us. We have to be open and ready for God to work in our hearts. We have to be willing to give God a fresh yes every day. We have to do what it takes according to God's instructions, not looking to the left or the right, but continuing to face forward. If we truly desire to experience destiny, we must always allow His word to be the lamp to our feet and the light to our path.

Destiny is promised to us all. We have to remind ourselves daily of our value and worth. God needs us to accomplish what He established in the earth. We have a job to do. Let's remain focused and steadfast. After all, we are destined to become amazing!

Destiny Steps

Ask Yourself…

- What can I do to remain victorious?
- How can I start or continue to live life as an overcomer?
- What does a destiny fulfilled look like for me?

YOUR DESTINY MOMENT

God has something amazing in store for all of us. Before He can deliver, there is some work we must do. For many of us, that work is internal. We need to change the way we think about ourselves. We have to undo the hurt from our past and allow freedom to take hold of our lives. God cannot deliver destiny into our hands if we continue to live a life bound in chains. We can't operate in purpose if we refuse to live victoriously. We must take action. Decide that today will be the day you live life as an overcomer. Make today the day you begin to live life in the overflow and the abundance of what God has promised to you. Choose to live life with purpose on purpose and march into destiny!

Epilogue

My path to destiny has been filled with highs & lows, ups & downs. I've learned that destiny will not pursue me; I must pursue it. I've discovered that the path of destiny is not an easy one nor is it for the faint at heart. My destiny demands that I take hold and never let go. God has continually shown me His greatness as I've learned to lean on and trust in Him. While I do not have all of the pieces needed to complete life's puzzle, destiny continues to hand me what I need with each step I take.

I've learned that every moment of my destiny demands that I overcome my past mistakes and insecurities. Destiny demands that I take hold of each moment and never let go. Destiny demands that in every moment, I embrace change and my uniqueness. Destiny demands that I understand I am fearfully and wonderfully made. Some won't understand. At times, even I won't understand, but that doesn't matter. What matters is that I march toward destiny with the heartbeat of God until I meet destiny face to face. Then, I will finally know who I am and the importance of my DESTINY MOMENTS!

Stay Connected

Thank you for purchasing *Destiny Moments*. LaMonika would like to connect with you! Below are a few ways you can stay posted on new book releases, book signings, and other engagements with LaMonika.

EMAIL lamonika@lamonikanicole.com

WEBSITE www.lamonikanicole.com

FACEBOOK LaMonika Nicole

INSTAGRAM lamonikanicole